The Source

EDUCATION & EMPLOYMENT

Williams Commercial Group, LLC

PO Box 2075

Broken Arrow, OK 74013

Ordering Information:

Quantity sales. Special discounts are available on quantity purchases by corporations, associations, and others.

For details, contact the publisher at the address above.

Orders by U.S. trade bookstores and wholesalers.

Call:

(888)654-3129

or visit

www.williamsrealty.org

ISBN 978-1-312-59077-9

9 781312 590779   90000

Contents

Introduction

You are the one through which the thing has come into being or from which it has been obtained to give, sell, or make available. You provide the thing that is wanted or needed by somebody or make up for deficiency, loss, or lack.

Great Prayer Starter

You are the supply, you are not looking for someone to give you a job, but you are looking to fill the demand or need they have placed on what you have to offer.

What do you have to offer? (Typing, singing, customer service, welding training, computer, baby, sitting)

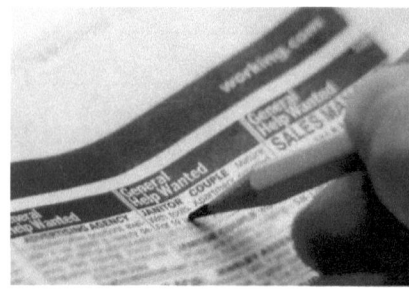

1._____

2._____

3._____

4._____

5._____

According to Webster Dictionary a demand is:

1. A forceful request: a clear and firm request that is difficult to ignore or deny.
2. The level of desire or need that exists for particular goods or services.
3. A need for resources or action.
4. An urgent requirement for time, facilities, resources, or action.

Did you know that when an employer places an ad in the paper they are making a request or sending a message? This is similar to when our nervous system sends a message to our brain, when we are upset or feeling rested, to produce a reaction that shows up outwardly through body movements or words. When the employer places an ad in the paper they want someone to respond with a supply that matches what they are requesting.

For instance, when you are relaxed, your nervous will generate a response that matches: relaxed, clear headed, and well-thought out. When you are anxious and upset you might generate the opposite.

Cerebral Cortex	Limbic System	Brain Stem
Humans	Humans, **Dogs & Cats**	Humans, Dogs & Cats, **Lizard & Snake**
Language: Easy Recall $4x + 2 = 10$ $X=2$	Emotions: I'm sad, when I think about what you did.	Sensations: The room is cold. The pen is hard.
Algebra	Memory	Hunger/Alertness/Temp Control
Relaxation Response	**Freeze, Fight or Flight response**	**Freeze, Fight or Flight Response**
Lower Heart Rates		

Have you tried to speak when you were angry? The words don't come out the same and tend to be the lowest form of vocabulary available to you at the time. This occurs because our heart rates are elevated.

When our heart rate is elevated our blood pressure is raised and this causes our nervous system to send signals to our brain that creates a physical reaction of a threat. When we are relaxed our physical reaction will display safety corresponding actions. The safety or threatened response we display has a major impact on our lives...

The response we give the employer should match the description of the message being displayed.

Contentment

CONTENTMENT IS A GREAT WAY TO DECREASE THE HEART RATE. ONE SURE WAY TO DEVELOP CONTENTMENT IS TO RECOGNIZE THE THINGS IN YOUR LIFE THAT YOU ARE GRATEFUL FOR.

NAME 10 THINGS THAT YOU ARE SO GRATEFUL FOR RIGHT NOW, TODAY........

1.

2.

3.

4.

5.

6.

7.

8.

9.

10.

EMPLOYMENT

Times have changed for job searching, and numerous websites are now available that post private industry jobs. Many companies also offer a way to apply online. However, these sites and new methods do not replace traditional and proven job-hunting approaches such as networking, personal contacts, business organizations, and interviewing.

EMPLOYMENT AGENCIES AND RECRUITERS

If you are looking for a job, you may come across ads from employment agencies or receive calls from recruiters that promise wonderful opportunities. While some companies honestly want to help you, others are more interested in taking your money. Be wary of:

- Promises to get you a job and a guaranteed income
- Up front fees, even when you are guaranteed a refund if
- you are dissatisfied
- Employment agencies whose ads read like job ads
- Promotions of "previously undisclosed" government jobs. All federal jobs are announced to the public at www.usajobs.gov.

Get a copy of the employment agency contract and review it carefully before you pay any money. Check with your local consumer protection agency and the Better Business Bureau to see whether any complaints have been filed about a company.

The Federal Trade Commission investigates businesses that fraudulently advertise employment openings and guarantee job placement. Contact the FTC if you have a complaint.

WORK-AT-HOME COMPANIES

Not all work-at-home opportunities deliver on their promises. Some classic work-at-home schemes are medical billing, envelope stuffing, and assembly or craftwork. Ads for these businesses say, "Be part of one of America's Fastest-Growing Industries. Earn thousands of dollars a month from your home!" Legitimate work-at- home program sponsors should tell you, in writing, what is involved in the program they are selling. Here are some questions you might ask a promoter:

- What tasks will I have to perform? (Ask the program sponsor to list every step of the job.)
- Will I be paid a salary, or will my pay be based on commission?

- Who will pay me?
- When will I get my first paycheck?
- What is the total cost of the work-at-home program, including supplies, equipment, and membership fees? What will I get for my money?

The answers to these questions may help you determine whether a work-at-home program is appropriate for your circumstances and whether it is legitimate.

Multilevel Marketing

Some multilevel marketing plans are legitimate; however, others are illegal pyramid schemes. In pyramids, commissions are based on the number of distributors recruited, rather than actual products that are sold.

If you are thinking about joining what appears to be a legitimate multilevel marketing plan, take time to learn about the plan:

- What is the company's track record?
- What products does it sell?
- Does it sell products to the public at large?
- Does it have the evidence to back up the claims it makes about its product?
- Is the product competitively priced?
- Is it likely to appeal to a large customer base?
- How much does it cost to join the plan?
- Are monthly minimum sales required to earn a commission?
- Will you be required to recruit new distributors to earn your commission?

PRE-EMPLOYMENT CREDIT CHECKS

Potential employers are not just reading your resume; they are also reviewing your credit history to find out:

- If you pay your bills on time.
- How much money you owe.
- If someone has sued you.

Potential employers must notify you and ask your permission before they request or use your credit report.

Be proactive and get a copy of your report before you begin your job search so you will know beforehand what companies see and correct inaccuracies.

If a company decides not to hire you because of your credit report, it must tell you so, as well as your rights to get a free report, and your rights to dispute the accuracy of the report.

Net-Based Business Opportunities

Many Internet business opportunities are scams that promise more than they can possibly deliver. These companies lure would-be entrepreneurs with false promises of big earnings for little effort. Some tips for finding a legitimate opportunity:

- Consider the promotion carefully.
- Study the business opportunity's franchise disclosure document.
- Get earnings claims in writing and compare them with the experience of previous franchise and business opportunity owners.
- Visit previous franchise and business opportunity owners in person, preferably at their places of business.
- Check out the company with the local consumer protection agency and Better Business Bureau to see whether there have been any complaints.
- If the business opportunity involves selling products from well-known companies, verify the relationship with the legal department of the company whose merchandise you would promote.
- Consult an attorney, accountant, or other business advisor before you put any money down or sign any papers.
- Take your time. Promoters of fraudulent business opportunities are likely to use high-pressure sales tactics to get you to buy in. If the business opportunity is legitimate, it will still be around when you are ready to decide.

Unemployment

The government's Unemployment Insurance Program provides benefits to eligible workers who become unemployed through no fault of their own and who meet other eligibility requirements. Each state administers its own program under federal guidelines. Eligibility requirements, benefit amounts, and length of benefits are determined by the states. For more information, go to www.dol.gov/dol/topic/unemployment-insurance/ index.htm. In addition, some states are extending unemployment benefits for eligible recipients for up to 13 additional weeks. Visit www.workforcesecurity.doleta.gov for the latest information regarding your state's benefit programs.

Interview Preparation

Keep your resume and job description before you During the interview.

Answer each question showing how your background meets the need for their demand.

Prepare answers ahead of time....they are usually the same and you can develop your style for answering as you practice

Study up on the organizations culture (Size, people, and work life)

Follow Up:
Thank You Letters- 24 hours after interview
Letters of Acknowledgement- sent to confirm interview

Interview Questions

Question 1: Can you tell me something about yourself?

    a.   The interview is really asking why did you apply for this demand

    b.   State in simple terms what you're supplying and how much you enjoy supplying it.

    c.   Basically what attracted you to the demand

Question 2: Why did you apply for this job?

    a.   The interviewer really wants to know if you know anything about the organization.

    b.   Show that you know about the organizations culture and why you fit well with where the company is heading

    c.   Talk about the organizations vision and mission statement

Question 3: Why did you leave your last job? / Why are you planning to leave your job?

    a.   Tell the truth. If you were fired. Tell why and how you have improved in that area.

    b.   If you quit. State why and what you learned from the situation.

Question 4: Can you tell me something about your education?

    a.   If you have education that relates to the position state how it fits with the position you're applying for.

    b.   If you have no education talk about your skills and how prepared you are to meet the demand.

Question 5: Can you tell us something more about your working experience?

    a.   Answer by expounding on the job history portion of your resume. The interview will appreciate not having to take so many notes.

    b.   Talk about how the skills you have developed in the job history meet the demand for what they are looking for.

Question 6: Why should we hire you?

    a.   Go back and summarize the job description by linking the demands they have can be met with the experience and job history from your resume.

    b.   Close strong by letting them know that you have the supply that meets their demand and are available to fill that order in an efficient and effective manner.

Question 7: What are your strengths?

    a.   Your strengths are going to be expressed based on the skills they listed in notice for the demand.

    b.   Two or Three responses will be plenty.

        "I am very responsible person and always accomplish all my duties."

        "I am a very organized person, what is strongly reflected in my work."

        "I have good communication skills. I believe that communication skills are crucial in every job, but especially in job like this one."

Question 8: What are your weaknesses?

    a.   Your weakness should be true and never do I have any. You being aware of weakness is a sign that you are growing. Never answer this question leaving a checkmark in the interviewers mind.

    b.   It's best to answer this question with your long term goal and what plans you have in place to

    c.   Improve the situation.

    d.   "I would like to increase my education and will start school in the fall to obtain a LPN license. I will take classes at night part."

Question 9: What are your goals in five years horizon?

    a.   You should be well prepared for this question. Make sure it's in line with the organization future plans and show that you know what direction the company is heading.

    b.   Every responsible person has some goals. Employers know this. When questioning you about your goals, they simply want to hear that you have any goals.

    c.   However, you can do a mistake here. Some people like to mention that they dream about their own business. This is not a good answer. Companies do not want to hire someone who leaves after two years to start his own business.

Question 10: What are your biggest achievements so far?

    a.   If you don't have a certificate to show. Talk about a work related situation that you became better at over the years.

    b.   How it makes you a better candidate.

    c.   "I became a better person over the years. I learned to listen to the others and see the good in people. I consider this as my biggest achievement."

Question 11: What characterize a good boss/ colleague from your point of view?

    a.   Keep it casual. You can work with any personality, you enjoy your work and know how to get along with others.

b. "I can get along with everyone. All I want to be sure about when it comes to my boss and colleagues is that they are qualified for the job. And when I see the level of proficiency in this interview, I am sure they are qualified."

c. "There is nothing like an ideal boss for me. I simply focus on my job and on my performance and try to avoid any conflicts with other employees."

Question 12: What motivates you? / How do you motivate the others?

a. You are there because you meet the demand. Obviously you enjoy supplying this demand. Let the interviewer know that.

b. "I want to feel important in my job, do a good job for my employer. This is very important for me, to see a purpose in my job. It naturally motivates me to work hard and try to become better every day."

c. "I just like to work. If I was not strongly motivated to do this job, I would not apply for it. I would never work only for money."

Question 13: What are your salary expectations?

a. Research average salary is for the type of job being offered. Always give a high low number and see what they come back at.

b. "First of all, salary is not a deciding factor for me. I really like the job description and want to get this job. I will accept an average salary for this position what is something between $35,000 and $40,000", according to my knowledge.

c. "I really like this job and would like to do it. I have looked at the average salaries and found out that the average is between $35,000 and $40,000 for this position. I am willing to accept the lower figure from this range, as I really like would like to have this job."

Question 14: When are you able to start?

a. "I am ready to start as soon as possible."

b. "There is a two months' notice period in my company. However, I have very good relations with my boss so I am sure I can negotiate it and start earlier."

c. "I could possibly start tomorrow, but I want to finish the project I currently work on. It will be very unprofessional and irresponsible from me to leave now. I will need two or three weeks. I hope you understand this."

Question 15: Do you have any questions?

a. "What are the next steps of the recruiting process?"

b. "Can you tell me something more about the working environment?"

c. "What are the goals of your company in long term horizon?"

Interview Etiquette
Day of Interview

1. Brush your teeth and use a mouthwash.

2. Your hair should be clean and combed.

3. Nails should be clean and trimmed.

4. Be conservative and err on the side of caution. If the company does not have a dress code, remember that it's better to over dress than under dress.

5. Men can look their professional best wearing one of the many men suits available to you today. Shirts should be clean and ironed. If in doubt, wear a classic, conservative tie.

6. Women can look their professional best with business attire.

7. Wear dress shoes. Your shoes should be clean and/or shined. Arrive at least 15 minutes before your interview. The extra minutes will also give time to fill out any forms or applications that might be required.

During the Interview

1. Make a positive and professional first impression by being assertive and giving a firm handshake to each interviewer and addressing each interviewer by name as he or she is introduced.

2. Smile. When you smile you'll look more relaxed and confident. Plus, you'll feel more relaxed.

3. Reinforce your professionalism and your ability to communicate effectively by speaking clearly and avoiding "us", "you knows", and slang.

4. Use appropriate working. You won't receive extra points for each work that has more than ten letters. Use technical terms only when appropriate to the question.

5. Ask questions. Your first question should not be "Do you validate parking?"

After the Interview

1. Shake each interviewer's hand and thank each interviewer by name

2. Send a thank you note (not an e-mail) as soon after the interview as possible.

Career Research

U.S. Bureau of Labor Statistics

Occupational Outlook

Job Search

- ☐ jobungo.com
- ☐ CareerBuilder.com (USA)
- ☐ Craigslist (by city)
- ☐ Dice.com (USA)
- ☐ Hotjobs.com (USA)
- ☐ Indeed.com (USA)
- ☐ Glassdoor.com (USA)
- ☐ LinkUp.com (USA)
- ☐ Monster.com (USA), (India)
- ☐ Yahoo! Hot Jobs (Countrywide subdomains, International)

Skill Supply Builder:

1. What actions or skills do you have to supply, today?

2. How much time can you supply, today?

3. How can you increase (gain or improve) your actions, skills, or product?

EDUCATION

The U.S. Department of Education's website, www.studentaid.ed.gov, provides information on preparing for and funding education beyond high school with details on federal aid programs. Another source of information on financial assistance is www.finaid.org. Both sites offer calculators to help you determine how much school will cost, how much you need to save, and how much aid you will need.

There are steps you can take as you plan for college expenses. Check the Department of Education's graphic that shows how to apply for financial aid and college at studentaid.gov/sites/default/files/financial-aid-process.png.

COLLEGE ACCREDITATION

Accreditation ensures that education provided by institutions of higher education meets acceptable levels of quality. The Secretary of Education is required by law to publish a list of nationally recognized accrediting agencies that it determines to be reliable authorities on the quality of education or training provided by the institutions of higher education and the higher education programs they accredit. You can access the list at www.ope.ed.gov/accreditation.

PAYING FOR COLLEGE 101

Many state governments have created 529 Plans that make it easier for families to save for their child's education. These plans, which can be sponsored by states or institutions of higher learning, encourage saving for future college costs, and the earnings grow tax-free. There are two main types: "prepaid tuition plans" and "college savings plans." Prepaid plans allow you to pay for your child's college tuition based on today's costs, and then pay out at the future (higher) cost once your child is in college.

College savings plans allow you to invest money in several investment funds, ranging in risk level, to pay for your child's college education. For more information about the different types of

529 Plans and the plans available in each state, visit www.collegesavings.org.

Financial Aid

Student financial aid is available from a variety of sources, including the federal government, individual states, colleges and universities, and other public and private agencies and organizations. The four basic types of college aid are:

- Grants. Gift aid that does not have to be repaid and is generally awarded according to financial need.
- Work-Study. The Federal Work-Study Program is a federally funded source of financial assistance used to offset financial education costs. Students who qualify earn money by working while attending school. This money does not have to be repaid.
- Loans. Funds are borrowed and must be repaid with interest. As a general rule, federal student loans have more favorable terms and lower interest rates than traditional consumer loans do.
- Scholarships. Funds are offered by the school, local/ community organizations, private institutions, and trusts. Scholarships do not have to be repaid and are generally awarded based on specific criteria.

Applying for Aid

You must complete and submit a Free Application for Federal Student Aid (FAFSASM) to apply for federal student aid. FAFSA on the Web is the quickest and easiest method of applying. Go to www.fafsa.gov to apply.

FEDERAL STUDENT AID

- You can order many helpful publications at www.edpubs.gov, or by calling 1-877-433-7827.

- The U.S. Department of Education's federal student aid website, www.studentaid.ed.gov.
- The National Association of Student Financial Aid Administrators provides advice, tips, and information on financing your education at www.nasfaa.org.

SCHOLARSHIP AND FINANCIAL AID SCAMS

Some companies offer to help you find scholarships, for a fee. If the company asks you for money up front, but does not deliver on its promises to find scholarships, it could be a scam. Red flags include:

- A "money-back guarantee." Unscrupulous companies attach conditions that make it impossible to get the refund.
- "Secret scholarships." Beware if a company claims to have inside knowledge of scholarship resources.
- Companies that charge ongoing "monthly" or "weekly" fees for their services.
- Remember, you can get free scholarship information from a school counselor, the library and the Department of Education.

Learn more about financial aid scams at www.studentaid.ed.gov/types/scams. If you have been the victim of a financial aid scam, report it to the Federal Trade Commission at www.ftc.gov/complaint.

Education Tax Benefits

The federal government allows you to receive tax credits, deductions, and savings plans that can help with your expenses for higher education. The tax credits can reduce the amount of income tax you have to pay, while deductions reduce the amount of your income that is taxable. Visit www.irs.gov/uac/Tax-Benefits-for-

Education:-Information- Center for information on specific types of credits and deductions.

The Federal Student Aid Information Center (FSAIC) can answer your federal student financial aid questions and can give you all the help you need for free. You can also use the FSAIC automated response system to find out whether your FAFSASM has been processed and to request a copy of your Student Aid Report. For FSAIC contact information.

Federal Loan Program Repayment Information

- Public Service Loan Forgiveness Program. Offers forgiveness for outstanding federal loans for individuals working full time in public service jobs.
- Income-Based Repayment Plan. Helps to make repaying education loans more affordable for low-income borrowers.
- Both programs offer generous benefits, but the rules may seem complex, so it is important to get all of the details. For more information on these programs as well as other repayment options:
- U.S. Department of Education/Federal Student Aid: www. studentaid.ed.gov/repay-loans.
- National Association of Student Financial Aid Administrators: www.nasfaa.org

Comparing Student Loans

The Consumer Financial Protection Bureau has a know before You Owe Student Loan website, www. consumerfinance.gov/paying-for-college/compare- financial aid and college-cost. This financial aid tool lets you compare financial aid offers from multiple colleges.

You can take steps to avoid defaulting on your student loan. Before you get the loan, determine how much money you need to borrow and only borrow that amount. When you get the loan, make certain that you understand the details such as the payment terms and what type of loan you have. Once your student loan becomes due:

- Maintain accurate records of your loan, including the loan agreement, interest rates, and account numbers.
- Track your loans to stay updated on how much you owe.
- Make certain that the loan servicer has your current contact and bank account information (if payments are withdrawn automatically).
- If you default, it means you failed to make payments on your student loan as scheduled. Your loan becomes delinquent the first day after you miss a payment. However, the loan is not in default until 270 days have passed without a payment. The consequences of default can be severe, including:
- The entire unpaid balance of your loan and any interest is immediately due and payable.
- Your loan account is assigned to a collection agency.
- The loan will be reported as delinquent to credit bureaus, damaging your credit rating.
- Your federal and state taxes may be withheld through a tax offset. This means that the Internal Revenue Service can take your federal and state tax refund to collect any of your defaulted student loan debt.
- Your employer can withhold money from your pay and send the money to the government. This process is called wage garnishment.

If you are having difficulty making your payments, contact your loan servicer immediately. The servicer may be able to help by changing your repayment plan, switching the due date, getting a deferment or forbearance, or consolidating your student loans.

For information to help you avoid defaulting, visit www.studentaid.ed.gov/repay-loans/default.

Brainstorm:

1. When I was young I loved to?

2. I am happiest when I?

3. If money wasn't an issue I would do?

4. I would like to meet the demand for?

5. I would make a difference in the lives of others by doing?

Schedule It

The most important part of accomplishing your

employment or educational goals is to schedule it and

write it down after you decide on the direction you will

take.

- *Keep your goals before you to help you stay accountable*
- *Let others know what you're doing and seek help when needed to help you stay accountable*
- *Set a start Date.*
- *Calculate how long it will take and how much time you can devote to it*

My main goal is:

_____

_____

_____

A mini-goal or objective I need to meet before I can
achieve that goal is:

_____

_____

_____

To achieve that mini-goal or objective, I need to:

_____

_____

_____

Name: _____

Date: _____

In the table below, record the resources and actions you use to achieve your objective.

Date	Action	Result

Date	Action	Result

Notes:

_____

_____

_____

_____

_____

Handouts:

Career Planning Worksheet

Cover Letter

Resume

Employment Application

Workbook

Education
&
Employment

180 TRAINING.NET

Career and Education Planning Worksheet

Name: _____ Date: _____

Congratulations on beginning to plan for your future! Complete this worksheet as you move through the Career Planning unit. As you complete each of the activities, you can transfer key information to this worksheet. When you finish, you will have a career and education plan to take with you. It will help you think about additional information you may need to gather from other sections of the website such as Applying to College and Financial Planning.

<u>**Self Exploration**</u>

I have the most experience doing this type of work (put a check mark beside the area in which you have the most experience.)

___Working with People   ___Working with Things   ___Working with Data

My top three skills are:

1. _____

2. _____

3. _____

My top three job and work values are:

1. _____

2. _____

3. _____

My top three interest areas are:

1. _____

2. _____

3. _____

Three occupations that I would like to explore further are:

1. _____

2. _____

3. _____

Occupational Exploration

For each of the three occupations you identified, complete the following section using the information you gathered.

Occupation #1: _____ Average Annual Salary: _____

Three things that a person in this type of occupation does: _____

_____

Three things that I know about the working conditions in this occupation: (For example, does it require working outside or indoors? Does it require sitting or standing all day?)

_____

This occupation matches my job values, interests, and skills in the following three ways:

_____

_____

Occupation #2: _____ Average Annual Salary: _____

Three things that a person in this type of occupation does: _____

_____

Three things that I know about the working conditions in this occupation: (For example, does it require working outside or indoors? Does it require sitting or standing all day?)

_____

This occupation matches my job values, interests, and skills in the following three ways:

_____

_____

Occupation #3: _____ Average Annual Salary: _____

Three things that a person in this type of occupation does: _____

_____

Three things that I know about the working conditions in this occupation: (For example, does it require working outside or indoors? Does it require sitting or standing all day?)

_____

This occupation matches my job values, interests, and skills in the following three ways:

_____

_____

Educational Planning

For the three occupations you identified, complete the following section using the information you gathered:

Occupation #1: _____

What training or degrees do you need for this career? _____
_____

What license, if any, do you need to work in this career? _____

What educational steps do you need to take to prepare for this career? _____
_____

Where will you get your education?_____

How long it will it take? _____What will it cost? _____

How will you pay for it? _____

Occupation #2: _____

What training or degrees do you need for this career? _____
_____

What license, if any, do you need to work in this career? _____

What educational steps do you need to take to prepare for this career? _____
_____

Where will you get your education?_____

How long it will it take? _____What will it cost? _____

How will you pay for it? _____

Occupation #3: _____

What training or degrees do you need for this career? _____
_____

What license, if any, do you need to work in this career? _____

What educational steps do you need to take to prepare for this career? _____
_____

Where will you get your education?_____

How long it will it take? _____What will it cost? _____

How will you pay for it? _____

My Career and Educational Goals

Short Term Goal (6 months - 1 year):_____

_____

Long Term Goal (2 - 5 years): _____

_____

Every long-term goal is made up of many short term goals and steps. As you get closer to your long-term goal, you will set new short term goals.

The steps I need to take now to reach my long-term goals are:

Step	Date to complete step
1.	
2.	
3.	
4.	

Functional Resume

[Your Name]
[Street Address]
[City, ST ZIP Code]
[Phone number]
[E-mail address]
[Website]

[Date]

[Recipient Name]
[Title]
[Company Name]
[Street Address]
[Street Address 2]
[City, ST ZIP Code]

Dear [Recipient Name]:

Are you looking for a [**job title**] with:

- [Number of years in the field] years of hands-on experience in [area of experience]?
- Knowledge of the latest technology in [industry or field]?
- Excellent written and oral communication skills?
- A passion to learn and to increase his skills?

If so, then you need look no further. You will see from my enclosed resume that I meet all of these qualifications and more.

I would very much like to discuss opportunities with [**Company Name**].To schedule an interview, please call me at [**your phone number**].The best time to reach me is between [**earliest time available**] and [**latest time available**], but you can leave a voice message at any time, and I will return your call.

Thank you for taking the time to review my resume. I look forward to talking with you.

Sincerely,

[**Your Name**]

Enclosure

Functional Resume

Janet Williams

[Address, City, ST ZIP Code] | [Telephone] | [Email]

Objective

· Check out the quick tips below to help you get started. To replace tip text with your own, just click it and start typing.

Education

[DEGREE] | [DATE EARNED] | [SCHOOL]

· Major: [Click here to enter text]
· Minor: [Click here to enter text]
· Related coursework: [Click here to enter text]

[DEGREE] | [DATE EARNED] | [SCHOOL]

· Major: [Click here to enter text]
· Minor: [Click here to enter text]
· Related coursework: [Click here to enter text]

Skills & Abilities

MANAGEMENT

· Need another experience or education entry? You got it. Just click in the second sample entry for either and then click the plus sign that appears.

SALES

· On the Design tab of the ribbon, check out the Themes, Colors, and Fonts galleries to get a custom look with just a click.
· Looking for a matching cover letter? All you had to do was ask! On the Insert tab, select Cover Page.

COMMUNICATION

· You delivered that big presentation to rave reviews. Don't be shy about it now! This is the place to show how well you work and play with others.

LEADERSHIP

· Are you president of your fraternity, head of the condo board, or a team lead for your favorite charity? You're a natural leader—tell it like it is!

Experience

[JOB TITLE] | [COMPANY] | [DATES FROM - TO]

· This is the place for a brief summary of your key responsibilities and most stellar accomplishments.

COMPANY NAME
Employment Application

APPLICANT INFORMATION

Last Name		First		M.I.	Date
Street Address				Apartment/Unit #	
City		State		ZIP	
Phone		E-mail Address			
Date Available		Social Security No.		Desired Salary	
Position Applied for					

Are you a citizen of the United States?	YES ☐	NO ☐	If no, are you authorized to work in the U.S.?	YES ☐ NO ☐
Have you ever worked for this company?	YES ☐	NO ☐	If so, when?	
Have you ever been convicted of a felony?	YES ☐	NO ☐	If yes, explain	

EDUCATION

High School			Address			
From	To	Did you graduate?	YES ☐	NO ☐	Degree	
College			Address			
From	To	Did you graduate?	YES ☐	NO ☐	Degree	
Other			Address			
From	To	Did you graduate?	YES ☐	NO ☐	Degree	

REFERENCES

Please list three professional references.

Full Name		Relationship	
Company		Phone	
Address			
Full Name		Relationship	
Company		Phone	
Address			
Full Name		Relationship	
Company		Phone	
Address			

PREVIOUS EMPLOYMENT

Company   Phone

Address   Supervisor

Job Title   Starting Salary $ Ending Salary $

Responsibilities

From   To   Reason for Leaving

May we contact your previous supervisor for a reference?   YES ☐   NO ☐

Company   Phone

Address   Supervisor

Job Title   Starting Salary $ Ending Salary $

Responsibilities

From   To   Reason for Leaving

May we contact your previous supervisor for a reference?   YES ☐   NO ☐

Company   Phone

Address   Supervisor

Job Title   Starting Salary $ Ending Salary $

Responsibilities

From   To   Reason for Leaving

May we contact your previous supervisor for a reference?   YES ☐   NO ☐

MILITARY SERVICE

Branch   From   To

Rank at Discharge   Type of Discharge

If other than honorable, explain

DISCLAIMER AND SIGNATURE

I certify that my answers are true and complete to the best of my knowledge.

If this application leads to employment, I understand that false or misleading information in my application or interview may result in my release.

Signature   Date

Brainstorm:

1. When I was young I loved to?

2. I am happiest when I?

3. If money wasn't an issue I would do?

4. I would like to meet the demand for?

5. I would make a difference in the lives of others by doing?

Schedule It

The most important part of accomplishing your employment or educational goals is to schedule it and write it down after you decide on the direction you will take.

- *Keep your goals before you to help you stay accountable.*
- *Let others know what you're doing and seek help when needed to help you stay accountable.*
- *Set a start Date*
- *Calculate how long it will take and how much time you can devote to it.*

My main goal is:

_____

_____

_____

A mini-goal or objective I need to meet before I can achieve that goal is:

_____

_____

_____

To achieve that mini-goal or objective, I need to:

_____

_____

_____

Name: _____

Date: _____

In the table below, record the resources and actions you use to achieve your objective.

Date	Action	Result

Date	Action	Result

Notes:

_____

_____

_____

_____

_____